IT'S NOT ABOUT
A PERFECT PERFORMANCE,
BUT A SINCERE HEART,
DRIVE, DETERMINATION,
AND STRENGTH.

—

MARY J. BLIGE

E
i
be
goes as planned.

—

ELI MANNING

You matter.
Your experiences
are a huge part of
the American story.

—

SELENA GOMEZ

PRACTICE
SOME FORM
OF COMPASSION
EVERY DAY.

—

RYAN REYNOLDS

CARPE *Every* DIEM

THE BEST GRADUATION ADVICE FROM
MORE THAN 100 COMMENCEMENT SPEECHES

ROBIE ROGGE

CLARKSON POTTER/PUBLISHERS
NEW YORK

SUBJECT	1	2	MIDTERM	3	4	FINAL
ENGLISH						
MATH						
SCIENCE						
LITERATURE						
PHILOSOPHY						
LANGUAGE						
PHYSICAL ED						
HISTORY						
MUSIC						
ART						
PSYCHOLOGY						

YOU WILL NEVER BE AS SMART AS YOU ARE TODAY. Tomorrow you will have more doubts. In ten years, even more. By forty you will think you know very little. By fifty you will be sure of it. By sixty you'll wish you were as certain as you were of things when you were fifty. And by seventy, you'll actually think dinnertime is three o'clock in the afternoon.

MITCH ALBOM, International School of Nice, 2008

TO THE SMARTEST GRADUATE:

_____

FROM:

_____

Okay, you've graduated. Commencement is over. But how will the rest of your life *commence*?

You could start with the advice here, distilled from over one hundred graduation speeches given by people who have been at the crossroads, like you, but have achieved enough success to be invited as commencement speakers. Your advisory board includes artists, academics, authors, and actors; presidents, poets, politicians, philanthropists, entrepreneurs, and community activists. They have won Nobel and Pulitzer Prizes, Presidential and Olympic Gold medals, as well as Oscars and Emmys.

In researching the best advice from these august speakers, we have discovered a variety of recommendations. Sometimes the suggestions are contradictory; sometimes they reach a similar conclusion but through different channels. We have carefully paired the advice for you to review and judge. (You *are,* after all, the graduate.)

From now on, you get to choose your own adventure. You decide what to make (Neil Gaiman) or what to wreck (John Waters); whether your perspective on the challenges of the environment is global (Paul Hawken) or personal (Kermit the Frog); and what you can learn from your failures (Conan O'Brien). Consider Russell Baker's ten ways to avoid making the world worse, David McCullough's list of what to read instead of watching television, the rules of success shared by self-made billionaire Robert F. Smith, and Ellen DeGeneres' suggestion of the best path to take.

Congratulations for being in a position to try out different paths and figure out where you want to go. And along the way you might just pick up enough wisdom to get your own invitation to be a commencement speaker someday.
Carpe every diem.

MICHAEL DELL

University of
Texas at Austin

2003

As you start your journey,
the first thing you should do is
throw away that store-bought
map and begin to draw your own.

Billionaire businessman and philanthropist **MICHAEL DELL** started his computer business in his freshman year at the University of Texas at Austin. He was so successful that he dropped out and built Dell Technologies into one of the largest technology infrastructure companies in the world.

JON BON JOVI
Rutgers University, Camden

2015

IT'S OKAY TO MAP OUT YOUR FUTURE—BUT DO IT IN PENCIL.

Singer-songwriter **JON BON JOVI** is the founder and frontman of the Grammy Award–winning rock band Bon Jovi. He is also an actor, the majority owner of a football team, and head of a charitable foundation that serves the homeless.

ADMIRAL WILLIAM H. McRAVEN

UNIVERSITY OF TEXAS AT AUSTIN

20 14

If you make your bed every morning you will have accomplished the first task of the day. It will give you a small sense of pride, and it will encourage you to do another task and another and another. By the end of the day, that one task completed will have turned into many tasks completed. Making your bed will also reinforce the fact that little things in life matter. If you can't do the little things right, you will never be able to do the big things right.

Four-star **ADMIRAL WILLIAM H. McRAVEN** returned to his alma mater to give advice based on his experience training to be a U.S. Navy SEAL. His first lesson was so original and doable that his speech became a bestselling book.

PATTI SMITH

Pratt Institute

2010

My greatest urge is to speak to you of dental care . . . you want at night to be pacing the floor because your muse is burning inside of you . . . [not] because you need a damn root canal. So, floss, salt, baking soda, get them professionally cleaned . . . Take care of your damned teeth.

PATTI SMITH is a singer-songwriter, musician, author, and poet who was influential in the New York City punk rock scene in the late 1970s and continues to perform today. Her memoir *Just Kids* won a National Book Award.

STEPHEN COLBERT

Wake Forest College

2015

And if there's one thing you need . . . it's your own set of standards. . . . Once you leave here, you may miss being graded. . . . From now on, you fill out your own report card. So do yourself a favor: Be an easy grader. Score yourself on a curve. Give yourself extra credit. You are your own professor now. . . . You have tenure. They can't fire you.

STEPHEN COLBERT (see also page 113) is a comedian, television host, writer, producer, and political commentator. Colbert compared a personal transition of his own to that of the class: it's time to say goodbye to the person we've become and to make some decisions about the person we want to be.

GEORGE W. BUSH
Yale University

2001

TO THOSE OF YOU WHO RECEIVED HONORS, AWARDS, AND DISTINCTIONS, I SAY, WELL DONE. AND TO THE "C" STUDENTS, I SAY, YOU, TOO, CAN BE PRESIDENT OF THE UNITED STATES.

GEORGE W. BUSH served as the forty-third president of the United States from 2001 to 2009. He returned to his alma mater to give this address.

GEORGE SAUNDERS

Syracuse University

2013

What I regret most in my life are failures of kindness. Those moments when another human being was there, in front of me, suffering, and I responded . . . sensibly. Reservedly. Mildly. . . . As a goal in life . . . Try to be kinder.

GEORGE SAUNDERS is an award-winning short story writer, novelist, essayist, and professor. His commencement speech was turned into a *New York Times* bestselling book, *Congratulations, by the Way: Some Thoughts on Kindness.*

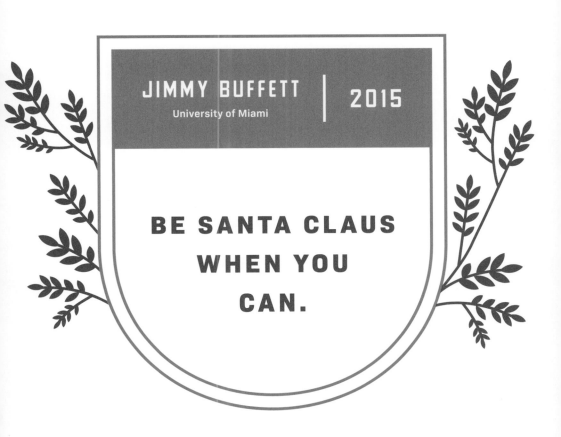

JIMMY BUFFETT | 2015
University of Miami

BE SANTA CLAUS WHEN YOU CAN.

Singer-songwriter, musician, and entrepreneur **JIMMY BUFFETT** gave his speech in flip-flops and offered a checklist of advice, including repaying the gift of your education by paying it forward.

TONI MORRISON

Wellesley College

2004

You are your own stories and therefore free to imagine and experience what it means to be human without wealth. What it feels like to be human without domination over others, without reckless arrogance, without fear of others unlike you, without rotating, rehearsing, and reinventing the hatreds you learned in the sandbox. And although you don't have complete control over the narrative—no author does, I can tell you—you could nevertheless create it.

TONI MORRISON was a novelist, essayist, editor, professor, and the recipient of the Nobel Prize for Literature, a Pulitzer Prize, and the Presidential Medal of Freedom. Her writing examines the experience of Black Americans, and she is one of the most celebrated authors in the country.

LIN-MANUEL MIRANDA

UNIVERSITY OF PENNSYLVANIA

20 16

Every story you choose to tell, by necessity, omits others from the larger narrative. . . . This act of choosing—the stories we tell versus the stories we leave out—will reverberate across the rest of your life.

LIN-MANUEL MIRANDA is a writer, composer, and performance artist probably best known for his Broadway production of *Hamilton: An American Musical.* He is also the recipient of Pulitzer, Grammy, Tony, and MacArthur Awards.

BARACK
OBAMA

Ohio State
University

2013

As Americans, we are blessed with God-given talents and inalienable rights . . . And as citizens, we understand that it's not about what America can do for us; it's about what can be done by us, together, through the hard and frustrating but absolutely necessary work of self-government.

BARACK OBAMA (see also page 123) was the forty-fourth president of the United States from 2009 to 2017, the first African American to serve. In this speech, he expressed concerns about our society's celebrating individual ambition above all else.

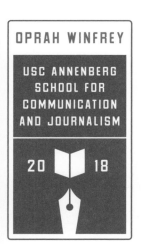

OPRAH WINFREY

USC ANNENBERG
SCHOOL FOR
COMMUNICATION
AND JOURNALISM

20 18

Vote! Vote! Vote! Pay attention to what the people who claim to represent you are doing and saying in your name and on your behalf. They represent you and if they've not done right by you, if their policies are at odds with your core beliefs, then you have a responsibility to send them packing.

OPRAH WINFREY (see also page 71) is a talk show host, actress, producer, media executive, and billionaire philanthropist. She urged the new generation of journalists and communication workers to fight fake news with facts, to capture the humanity of the stories they tell, and to avoid cynicism at all costs.

DON'T WALK DOWN THE GRAND CANYON TO SEE WHAT IT LOOKS LIKE FROM THE BOTTOM.

DON'T SMOKE AND DON'T VAPE.

NOTHING LOOKS BETTER IN YOUR FIFTIES THAN SUNSCREEN IN YOUR TWENTIES.

WHEN IT COMES TO HALLOWEEN COSTUMES, GO FUNNY OVER SEXY.

MIXED SIGNALS ARE NOT MIXED SIGNALS—

IMPOSE SELF-DISCIPLINE AROUND THREE THINGS: HAVE A BOOK ON YOUR BEDSIDE TABLE AT ALL TIMES. . . . BE IN CHARGE OF YOUR CONSUMPTION OF SOCIAL MEDIA. AND FOSTER A SENSE OF HUMOR ABOUT YOURSELVES.

IF YOU'RE A WOMAN . . . THE WORLD IS YOURS TO GRAB. GO OUT AND GET IT, GIRL.

FINALLY, STAY CLOSE TO YOUR FRIENDS FROM COLLEGE.

THEY'RE A NO.

Actress and entrepreneur **JENNIFER GARNER** returned to her college, advising graduates to insist on optimism to see them through their day-to-day living. Garner also gave them tips from what she had learned.

When I think of the men and women I most admire, one quality they share is a willingness to work and sacrifice for great and difficult things . . . There is no stronger motivation than knowing that when you're not practicing, someone else is.

MICHELLE KWAN is the most decorated figure skater in the United States. She is a two-time Olympic medalist, a five-time world champion, and a nine-time U.S. champion. When she gave this speech, she had retired from skating and was a student herself.

ANNA QUINDLEN
Villanova University

2000

DON'T EVER CONFUSE
THE TWO, YOUR LIFE
AND YOUR WORK. THE
SECOND IS ONLY PART
OF THE FIRST.

ANNA QUINDLEN (see also pages 65 and 103) is a Pulitzer Prize–winning journalist and a bestselling author of fiction and nonfiction. Because of student protests at this Catholic university, Quindlen did not get to deliver the speech, but she later expanded it in a book, *A Short Guide to a Happy Life.*

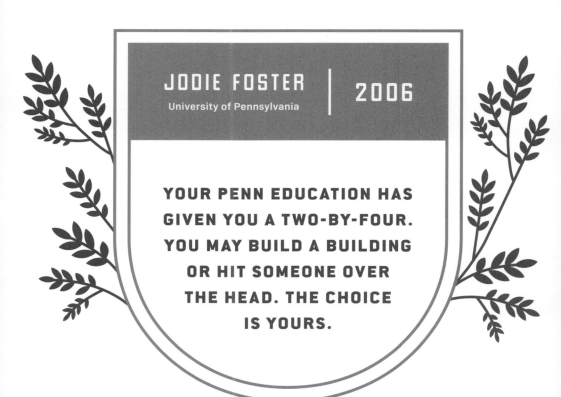

JODIE FOSTER | 2006
University of Pennsylvania

YOUR PENN EDUCATION HAS GIVEN YOU A TWO-BY-FOUR. YOU MAY BUILD A BUILDING OR HIT SOMEONE OVER THE HEAD. THE CHOICE IS YOURS.

JODIE FOSTER is an Academy Award–winning actress, director, and producer who started her acting career when she was three years old. She acted in many films before she slowed down at age eighteen to go to college.

BONO

University of
Pennsylvania

2004

The world is more malleable than you think, and it's waiting for you to hammer it into shape. . . . So go forth and build something with [this degree] . . . this is the time for bold measures and this is the country and you are the generation.

Singer-songwriter, musician, and U2 frontman **BONO** never went to college, but he studied rock and roll, which he said woke him up to the world. He became an equal-rights activist and philanthropist, especially interested in Africa.

PAUL
HAWKEN

University
of Portland

2009

You are going to have to figure out what it means to be a human being on earth at a time when every living system is declining, and the rate of decline is accelerating. . . . Important rules like don't poison the water, soil, or air, don't let the earth get overcrowded, and don't touch the thermostat have been broken.

Inspiration . . . resides in humanity's willingness to restore, redress, reform, rebuild, recover, re-imagine, and reconsider.

PAUL HAWKEN is an environmentalist, entrepreneur, journalist, and author. He has dedicated his life to environmental sustainability and improving the relationship between business and the environment. PBS named this commencement speech the best of the year.

KERMIT THE FROG
Southampton College

| 1996

ON BEHALF OF FROGS,
FISH, PIGS, BEARS, AND ALL
OF THE OTHER SPECIES WHO
ARE LOWER THAN YOU ON THE
FOOD CHAIN, THANK YOU FOR
DEDICATING YOUR LIVES TO
SAVING OUR WORLD AND
OUR HOME.

KERMIT THE FROG, the beloved green Muppet, received a Doctorate of Amphibious Letters at a college known for its emphasis on environmental studies. Due to his prominent role on *Sesame Street,* Kermit was recognized as one of the graduates' first teachers.

CHIMAMANDA NGOZI ADICHIE

AMERICAN
UNIVERSITY
COLLEGE OF ARTS
AND SCIENCES

20 19

Life is short really means do something. . . . Life is short really means have a purpose. And purpose does not need to be grand. I think that the smaller the purpose the more meaningful. To be kind. To have empathy. To avoid sanctimony. To think of the humanity of other people—to try.

CHIMAMANDA NGOZI ADICHIE is a writer of short stories, novels, and nonfiction who divides her time between Nigeria and the United States. She describes herself as a feminist in the way she looks at the world.

RACHEL MADDOW

Smith College

———

2010

Frankly, if all goes well, life is long. So if you might take advice from me I would offer this . . . Do stuff you will enjoy thinking about and telling stories about for many years to come. Do stuff you will want to brag about.

RACHEL MADDOW is an author, Rhodes Scholar, liberal political commentator, and host of the television program *The Rachel Maddow Show*. She urged graduates to aim for glory over fame and for long-term commitment to their nation versus short-term commitment to themselves.

NOTHING REPLACES ACTUALLY DOING THE WORK.

TAKE THOUGHTFUL RISKS.

YOU ARE ENOUGH.

WE ALL HAVE RESPONSIBILITY TO LIBERATE OTHERS.

ROBERT F. SMITH
Morehouse College
2019

BE INTENTIONAL ABOUT THE WORDS YOU CHOOSE.

ROBERT F. SMITH is a self-made billionaire and the richest Black man in America. He surprised the administration and graduates of this historically Black college by providing a grant to eliminate all student loans from this class. He expects the class to pay it forward and hopes his example will inspire the same opportunity for other classes. Smith shared specific rules to live by in attaining the American Dream.

MATTHEW
McCONAUGHEY

University of
Houston

2016

Look, the first step that leads to our identity in life is usually not I know who I am. . . . That's not the first step. The first step is usually, I know who I am not. Process of elimination. Defining ourselves by what we are not is the first step that leads us to really knowing who we are.

MATTHEW McCONAUGHEY is an actor and producer. He won an Oscar and a Golden Globe Award for his role in *Dallas Buyers Club*. In this speech he shared some of the things he has learned: life is not easy or fair, happiness demands an outcome but joy is constant, and nothing is "unbelievable."

JOSS WHEDON
WESLEYAN
UNIVERSITY
20 13

For your entire life, you will be doing, on some level, the opposite— not only of what you were doing— but of what you think you are. . . . To accept duality is to earn identity. And identity is something that you are constantly earning. It is not just who you are. It is a process that you must be active in.

JOSS WHEDON is a producer, director, screenwriter, comic book writer, and composer best known for his television series *Buffy the Vampire Slayer, Firefly,* and *Agents of S.H.I.E.L.D.,* as well as his Avengers movies and *The Cabin in the Woods*. He addressed graduates from his alma mater, talking about contradictions and connections.

JAMAICA KINCAID

Grinnell College | 2012

> YOU MUST BITE THE HAND THAT FEEDS YOU. . . . THE OPPOSITE OF THIS IS OFTEN SAID TO YOU, "DO NOT BITE THE HAND THAT FEEDS YOU." . . . BUT IT SEEMS TO ME THAT YOU MUST BITE THAT HAND, FOR HOW ELSE WILL YOU KNOW WHO YOU ARE, WHO YOU TRULY ARE?

JAMAICA KINCAID is a novelist, essayist, professor, and gardening writer who explores family ties and life in Antigua. Kincaid's difficult relationship with her mother has informed her writing.

CHANCE THE RAPPER

Dillard University

2018

The highest form of respect that we can pay to the people who came before us, the people who sacrificed for us and gave us everything, is to be better than them. . . . Our parents, grandparents, ancestors sacrificed, not so that we can keep doing the same thing that they were doing but so that we can be better. To simply copy them would be almost an insult to their sacrifice.

Grammy Award winner **CHANCE THE RAPPER** is a singer, songwriter, actor, and activist. He shared this insight after seeing Beyoncé at Coachella, where her performance surpassed even that of his hero Michael Jackson.

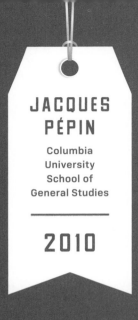

JACQUES
PÉPIN

Columbia
University
School of
General Studies

2010

Success in life is to be happy . . . with what you do. If you love what you do, you never have to go to work. Money for the sake of money doesn't make a person happy, although it may contribute to it a fair amount. Don't forget the simple pleasures of life. For me, it is still sharing a meal or a bottle of wine with friends, the enjoyment of being with families and friends. To share. This is true happiness.

JACQUES PÉPIN is a French-born American chef, television host, prolific author, teacher, and artist. Although he left school at age thirteen to apprentice in a kitchen and came to America at twenty-three, knowing very little English, he simultaneously pursued his education and his culinary career.

JOSÉ ANDRÉS

GEORGE WASHINGTON UNIVERSITY

20 14

There will always be critics and naysayers telling you what you cannot do. . . . But let me tell you: Get a cocktail shaker. Add your heart, your soul, your brain, your instinct, and shake it hard. Serve it straight up. But let me give you a secret ingredient: Add a dash of criticism on top because those naysayers play an important role, too. They motivate you to rise above, to challenge yourself, to prove them wrong.

JOSÉ ANDRÉS is a Spanish-born American chef who is credited with introducing Americans to both traditional and innovative Spanish cuisine. He is the founder of World Central Kitchen, a nonprofit that provides meals in the wake of disasters.

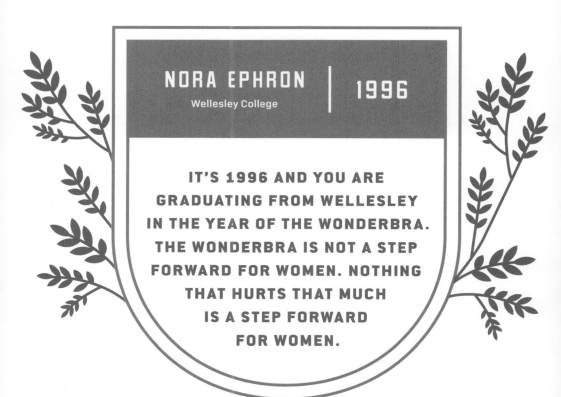

NORA EPHRON
Wellesley College

1996

IT'S 1996 AND YOU ARE GRADUATING FROM WELLESLEY IN THE YEAR OF THE WONDERBRA. THE WONDERBRA IS NOT A STEP FORWARD FOR WOMEN. NOTHING THAT HURTS THAT MUCH IS A STEP FORWARD FOR WOMEN.

NORA EPHRON, author, humorist, movie director, and feminist, graduated from Wellesley in 1962. Her commencement address thirty-four years later acknowledged some success of the women's movement, but Ephron urged graduates to continue the fight.

DOLLY PARTON

University of Tennessee

———

2009

Now, I usually try not to give advice. Information, yes, advice, no. But what has worked for me may not work for you. Well, take for instance what has worked for me. Wigs. Tight clothes, push-up bras, and high heel shoes.

DOLLY PARTON is a country music singer-songwriter, multi-instrumentalist, actress, entrepreneur, and philanthropist. She is also known for her distinct flamboyant style.

1. **ZERO IN ON BEING PRECISE WITH YOUR LANGUAGE.**
   The purpose is to enable you to articulate yourselves as fully and precisely as possible.

2. **TRY TO BE KIND TO YOUR PARENTS.**
   In all likelihood, they will die before you do, so you can spare yourselves at least this source of guilt if not of grief.

3. **TRY NOT TO SET TOO MUCH STORE BY POLITICIANS.**
   Because of the size of their job, which is too big even for the best . . . [all they can do] is to diminish a social evil, not eradicate it. . . . You ought to rely . . . on managing the world yourselves.

4. **TRY NOT TO STAND OUT.**
Try to be modest.

5. **AT ALL COSTS, TRY TO AVOID GRANTING YOURSELF THE STATUS OF THE VICTIM.**
The moment that you place blame somewhere, you undermine your resolve to change anything.

6. **TRY NOT TO PAY ATTENTION TO THOSE WHO WILL TRY TO MAKE LIFE MISERABLE FOR YOU.**
Suffer them if you can't escape them, but once you have steered clear of them, give them the shortest shrift possible.

JOSEPH BRODSKY was a poet, essayist, and professor, winner of the Nobel Prize for Literature in 1987, and United States Poet Laureate in 1991. He described life as a game with many rules—but no referee—that you learn to play by watching. He offered six tips for being a winner.

SHONDA RHIMES

DARTMOUTH COLLEGE

20 14

Ditch the dream and be a doer, not a dreamer . . . keep moving forward. You just have to keep doing something, seizing the next opportunity, staying open to trying something new. It doesn't have to fit your vision of the perfect job or the perfect life. Perfect is boring and dreams are not real. Just . . . do.

SHONDA RHIMES is an acclaimed television and film writer and producer best known for the TV series *Grey's Anatomy, Scandal,* and *How to Get Away with Murder.* Her address was given twenty years after her own graduation from Dartmouth.

ELLEN JOHNSON
SIRLEAF | 2011

Harvard University

IF YOUR DREAMS DO NOT SCARE YOU, THEY ARE NOT BIG ENOUGH.

Speaking at her alma mater, **ELLEN JOHNSON SIRLEAF** described her path to the presidency of Liberia, which included prison, death threats, and exile. She became the first elected female of the African continent, transforming the war-torn Liberia into a country of peace, development, and hope.

DAVID
REMNICK

Syracuse University

2014

All of us have 20/20 vision when it comes to the outrages of the past. . . . We look back on all this now with a self-satisfied notion that we are beyond such cruelties. . . . We are so far beyond them that we cannot imagine a moral sensibility that condoned and defended them. But . . . what conditions do we tolerate now that require our, your, visionary capacity and effort? What will we look back on with incredulous shame and how will we begin to right it? What gnaws at you? And what will you do about it?

DAVID REMNICK is a Pulitzer Prize–winning author and journalist and the current editor of *The New Yorker*. In his speech, he urged graduates to look beyond their own houses to identify the wrongs that exist in the world today.

SIDDHARTHA MUKHERJEE

UNIVERSITY OF SOUTHERN CALIFORNIA

20 18

"History doesn't repeat itself, but it rhymes" is a quote attributed, perhaps apocryphally, to Mark Twain. To understand that rhyme— to comprehend the parts that come back, but with a slightly altered lilt, a slightly altered tone or emphasis—is also a profound form of listening.

SIDDHARTHA MUKHERJEE is an oncologist, a biologist, and the Pulitzer Prize–winning author of *The Emperor of All Maladies: A Biography of Cancer*. He urged the graduates to listen to another mind, to listen to nature, and to listen to history.

STEVEN SPIELBERG

HARVARD UNIVERSITY

20 16

And please stay connected. Please never lose eye contact. This may not be a lesson you want to hear from a person who creates media, but we are spending more time looking down at our devices than we are looking in each other's eyes. . . . Please find someone's eyes to look into. . . . Just let your eyes meet. That's it. That emotion you're feeling is our shared humanity mixed in with a little social discomfort.

But, if you remember nothing else from today, I hope you remember this moment of human connection.

STEVEN SPIELBERG is one of the most popular and successful film directors, writers, and producers in the world. Although his job is to create a world that lasts two hours, he urged the graduates to create a world that lasts forever.

AMY POEHLER

Harvard University

2011

The answer to a lot of your life's questions is often in someone else's face. Try putting your iPhones down and look in people's faces. People's faces will tell you amazing things. Like if they're hungry, nauseous, or asleep.

AMY POEHLER (see also page 64) is an actress, comedian, writer, producer, and director, best known for her television work on *Saturday Night Live* and *Parks and Recreation*.

NEIL GAIMAN

UNIVERSITY
OF THE ARTS

20 12

When things get tough, this is what you should do. Make good art. . . . Leg crushed and then eaten by mutated boa constrictor? Make good art. IRS on your trail? Make good art. Cat exploded? Make good art. Do what only you do best. Make good art.

NEIL GAIMAN (see also page 96) is an author, poet, filmmaker, and a comic book and recording artist. The British multi-hyphenate told his graduates they had a unique talent. Whatever discipline—music, photography, fine art, cartoons, writing, design—they had the ability to make art.

JOHN WATERS
Rhode Island School of Design | 2015

CONTEMPORARY ART'S JOB IS TO WRECK WHAT CAME BEFORE. . . . GO OUT IN THE WORLD AND F—K IT UP BEAUTIFULLY. . . . HORRIFY US WITH *NEW* IDEAS. . . . IT'S YOUR TURN TO CAUSE TROUBLE— BUT THIS TIME IN THE REAL WORLD, AND THIS TIME FROM THE INSIDE.

JOHN WATERS is a filmmaker, director, actor, writer, and artist. When Waters gave his speech, he bragged about his qualifications: suspended from high school, kicked out of college, arrested many times, and awarded by the press with the title "The Prince of Puke."

1. TRY NOT TO GET A REGULAR JOB.

2. ALWAYS KEEP PEOPLE IN YOUR LIFE WHO DON'T QUITE UNDERSTAND WHAT YOU DO.

3. KEEP THE FRIENDS YOU MADE IN COLLEGE.

4. DO NOT JUDGE YOUR OWN SUCCESS BY THE SUCCESS OF OTHERS.

5. NEVER TURN DOWN A JOB BECAUSE OF MONEY.

6. IF YOU CAN'T GET IN THE FRONT DOOR, GO IN THE BACK DOOR.

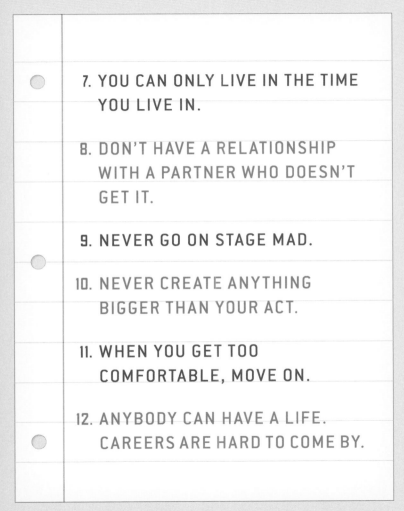

7. YOU CAN ONLY LIVE IN THE TIME YOU LIVE IN.

8. DON'T HAVE A RELATIONSHIP WITH A PARTNER WHO DOESN'T GET IT.

9. NEVER GO ON STAGE MAD.

10. NEVER CREATE ANYTHING BIGGER THAN YOUR ACT.

11. WHEN YOU GET TOO COMFORTABLE, MOVE ON.

12. ANYBODY CAN HAVE A LIFE. CAREERS ARE HARD TO COME BY.

When comedian and former late-night television host **JAY LENO** returned to his alma mater, he acknowledged that the school had saved him. His years at college were the first time being funny gave him something other than detention. Leno went on to share what he learned from show business. Here are the highlights.

BARBARA BUSH

Wellesley College

———————

1990

As important as your obligations as a doctor, lawyer, or business leader will be, you are a human being first, and those human connections—with spouses, with children, with friends—are the most important investments you will ever make. . . . Your success as a family—our success as a society—depends not on what happens in the White House, but on what happens inside your house.

BARBARA BUSH was first lady of the United States from 1989 to 1993, when her husband, George H. W. Bush, was the forty-first president. She was also the mother of George W. Bush, who served as the forty-third president from 2001 to 2009.

GEORGE H.W.
BUSH

UNIVERSITY OF
NOTRE DAME

19 92

Whatever form our most pressing problems take, ultimately, all are related to the disintegration of the American family. . . . Today's crisis will have to be addressed by millions of Americans at the personal, individual level for governmental programs to be effective. . . . The Federal Government, of course, must do everything it can do, but the point is, government alone is simply not enough.

GEORGE H.W. BUSH was a politician and businessman who was president of the United States from 1989 to 1993. He was married to Barbara Bush for over seventy years. At his death, his son George W. Bush said he was "a man of the highest character and the best dad a son or daughter could ask for."

VALERIE JARRETT

Wellesley College

2013

If you are willing to be flexible, you will find your true passion. So don't restrict your options, and limit your potential, with arbitrary, self-imposed deadlines. . . . Do not blindly ignore opportunities to change course, and certainly do not let others impose their priorities on you.

VALERIE JARRETT is a lawyer, businesswoman, politician, and author who served as a senior advisor to President Barack Obama. She followed her "plan" after she graduated, but she was miserable. She found happiness by leaving her cushy job and going into public service.

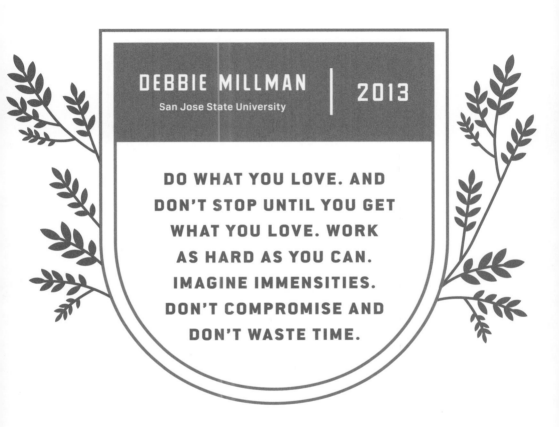

DEBBIE MILLMAN | 2013

San Jose State University

DO WHAT YOU LOVE. AND
DON'T STOP UNTIL YOU GET
WHAT YOU LOVE. WORK
AS HARD AS YOU CAN.
IMAGINE IMMENSITIES.
DON'T COMPROMISE AND
DON'T WASTE TIME.

DEBBIE MILLMAN is a writer, designer, educator, artist, and curator. She is best known as the host of the podcast *Design Matters,* where she delves into the lives of very creative people.

ATUL
GAWANDE

Williams College

2012

Scientists have given a new name to the deaths that occur in surgery after something goes wrong. . . . They call them a "Failure to Rescue." More than anything, this is what distinguished the great from the mediocre. They didn't fail less. They rescued more. . . . A failure often does not have to be a failure at all. However, you have to be ready for it. . . . The difference between triumph and defeat, you'll find, isn't about willingness to take risks. It's about mastery of rescue.

ATUL GAWANDE is a surgeon, writer, public health researcher, and professor. He was both a Rhodes Scholar and a MacArthur Fellow. Although speakers usually admonish graduates to take risks and not be afraid of failure, he admitted it is different in medicine.

KUMAIL NANJIANI

Grinnell College

———

2017

Nobody is paying attention to your failure. The world is full of people failing. People are failing all around you. Failure is boring. Your failure will not be so spectacular that people will write articles about your failure. Only you will remember your failure. Unless you're the person that made the Samsung Galaxy S7. Those are the phones that literally explode. Everyone knows that person's failure.

KUMAIL NANJIANI is a comedian, actor, podcast host, and writer who left his native Pakistan to attend this college in Iowa. He wrote and played himself in the romantic comedy *The Big Sick* and was a cast member in the TV series *Silicon Valley*.

BILL NYE

UNIVERSITY OF
MASSACHUSETTS,
LOWELL

20 14

Everyone you will ever meet knows something that you don't. . . . Respect their knowledge and learn from them. It will bring out the best in all of you.

BILL NYE is a scientist, engineer, comedian, author, and inventor best known as Bill Nye the Science Guy. He believes that thinking like a nerd is the key to improving yourself and your world.

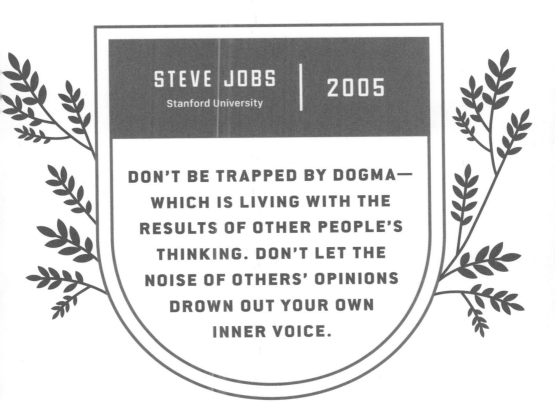

STEVE JOBS | 2005

Stanford University

DON'T BE TRAPPED BY DOGMA—
WHICH IS LIVING WITH THE
RESULTS OF OTHER PEOPLE'S
THINKING. DON'T LET THE
NOISE OF OTHERS' OPINIONS
DROWN OUT YOUR OWN
INNER VOICE.

STEVE JOBS was the co-designer of the Apple computer. He built his company, Apple Inc., into a world leader in telecommunication, tech innovation, and design. Jobs is responsible for the iPhone, among other advances in industrial design.

1. PINPOINT YOUR PASSION.

2. NO JOB IS BENEATH YOU.

3. WHO YOU WORK FOR AND WITH IS AS IMPORTANT AS WHAT YOU DO.

04 BE WILLING TO FAIL.

6. YOUR BEHAVIOR HAS CONSEQUENCES.

7. CHILDREN DO CHANGE YOUR CAREER.

8. MARRIAGE IS HARD WORK.

9. DON'T EXPECT ANYONE ELSE TO SUPPORT YOU FINANCIALLY.

10. LAUGHTER AND A SENSE OF HUMOR ABOUT YOURSELF WILL SMOOTH THE ROAD BEFORE YOU.

MARIA SHRIVER
College of the Holy Cross
1998

05 SUPERWOMAN IS DEAD.

MARIA SHRIVER is an author and an Emmy and Peabody Award–winning broadcast journalist. Shriver shared her observations from the fighting front of a graduate making it day-to-day in the real world. Her tips were expanded into a book, *Ten Things I Wish I'd Known— Before I Went Out into the Real World.*

BILLY JOEL

BERKLEE COLLEGE
OF MUSIC

19 93

I have said before to those who have expressed doubts and misgivings about their ability to live this kind of life, maybe they shouldn't try, because being a musician is not something you chose to be, it is something you are, like tall or short or straight or gay. There is no choice, either you is or you ain't.

BILLY JOEL is a singer-songwriter, composer, and pianist. He started piano lessons at an early age and dropped out of high school to pursue a musical career. He has sold more than 150 million records, making him one of the most popular entertainers in the world.

ROBERT DE NIRO

New York University,
Tisch School of the Arts

2015

WHEN IT COMES TO THE ARTS, PASSION SHOULD ALWAYS TRUMP COMMON SENSE. . . . YEAH, YOU'RE F—KED. THE GOOD NEWS IS, THAT'S NOT A BAD PLACE TO START.

ROBERT DE NIRO is an Academy Award–winning actor, producer, and director who has appeared in more than one hundred films in his career.

WILL FERRELL

University of Southern California

2017

After my first show, one reviewer referred to me as "the most annoying newcomer of the new cast." Someone showed this to me and I promptly put it up on the wall in my office, reminding myself that to some people I will be annoying. Some people will not think I'm funny, and that that's okay.

WILL FERRELL is a comedian, actor, and producer who first came to prominence as a cast member on *Saturday Night Live*. This address at his alma mater ended with his resounding performance of "I Will Always Love You."

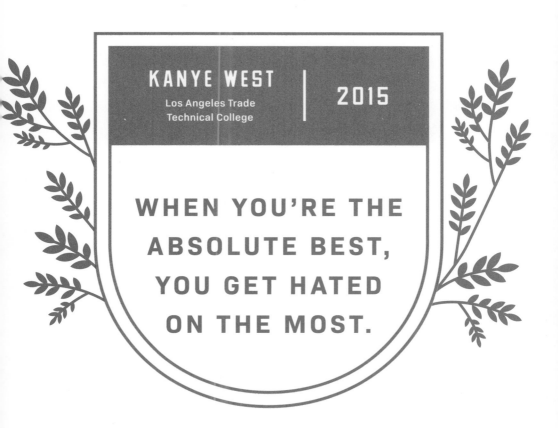

KANYE WEST

Los Angeles Trade
Technical College

2015

WHEN YOU'RE THE
ABSOLUTE BEST,
YOU GET HATED
ON THE MOST.

KAYNE WEST is a rapper, songwriter, producer, and fashion designer who has won more Grammys than any other rapper. The flamboyant West characterizes himself as a pop artist whose medium is public opinion and whose world is his canvas.

AMY POEHLER

HARVARD UNIVERSITY

20 11

You can't do it alone. As you navigate the rest of your life, be open to collaboration. Other people and other people's ideas are often better. Find a group of people who challenge and inspire you . . . and it will change your life.

AMY POEHLER (see also page 45) referred to her experience doing improvisation, from which she learned the importance of collaboration. She also urged the graduates to be nicer to their parents—"less eye-rolling."

ANNA
QUINDLEN

Mount Holyoke
College

———

1999

This is the hard work of your life in the world, to make it all up as you go along. . . . You will have to bend all your will not to march to the music that all of those great "theys" out there pipe on their flutes. . . . Each of you is as different as your fingerprints. Why in the world should you march to any lockstep?

ANNA QUINDLEN (see also pages 21 and 103) implored the class to give up the "nonsensical and punishing quest for perfection" that distracts too many through too much of our lives.

RONAN FARROW

LOYOLA MARYMOUNT UNIVERSITY

20 18

You will face a moment in your career where you have *absolutely no idea* what to do. . . . And I hope that in that moment you'll be generous with yourself, but trust that inner voice. Because more than ever we need people to be guided by their own senses of principle—and not the whims of a culture that prizes ambition, and sensationalism, and celebrity, and vulgarity, and doing whatever it takes to win.

Pulitzer Prize–winning journalist **RONAN FARROW** pursued a story that led to the indictment and conviction of movie mogul Harvey Weinstein and to the explosion of the international #MeToo movement. Farrow had to leave his job to get the story published.

GLORIA STEINEM
Bennington College

2015

IF IT LOOKS LIKE A DUCK AND WALKS LIKE A DUCK AND QUACKS LIKE A DUCK BUT YOU THINK IT'S A PIG, IT'S A PIG. TRUST YOUR INSTINCT.

GLORIA STEINEM is a feminist icon, journalist, social political activist, and a founder of *New York* and *Ms.* magazines. She offered graduates a list of her best advice, urging laughter, kindness, living in the present, equality, and self-confidence.

University
of California at
Berkeley, School
of Journalism

2014

○ **SOMEONE WHO IS UNDERESTIMATED WILL
BE THE ONE WHO CHANGES THE WORLD.**
It's not the person everyone expects. It might be you.

DO WHAT IS IN FRONT OF YOU.
Focus on the small steps ahead of you.

**DON'T WORRY ABOUT ACHIEVING
A MASTER PLAN, ABOUT THE PLOT TO
TAKE OVER THE WORLD.**

○ **BE A WORKER AMONG WORKERS.**
It's more important that you fit in before you stick out.

FOLLOW THE "MOM RULE."
Don't do anything you couldn't explain or justify
to your mom.

DON'T JUST DO WHAT YOU'RE GOOD AT.
Get outside of your comfort zone. Being a journalist
is permission for lifetime learning.

BE PRESENT.
Don't worry about documenting the moment with your smartphone. Experience it yourself.

TAKE RESPONSIBILITY FOR THE GOOD AND THE BAD.
Learn to own your failures.

BE HONEST.
Have the difficult conversation.

DON'T BE AFRAID TO BE AMBITIOUS.

Journalist **DAVID CARR** took seven years to get through college and spent time in rehab and on welfare before he went to work writing for the *New York Times*. He wrote the Media Equation column, which focused on the intersection of media and technology. Carr gave ten bits of advice to these future journalists.

KAMALA
HARRIS

Howard University

———

2017

Speaking the truth is different from telling the truth. Telling the truth means separating fact from fiction. . . . But unlike telling the truth, speaking the truth means you must speak up and speak out. Even when you're not being asked, and even when it's uncomfortable or inconvenient.

KAMALA HARRIS is a lawyer and politician who served as California's third female senator and the first of either Jamaican or Indian ancestry. In 2020, Harris became the first woman of color to be nominated for vice president of the United States. She shared her concerns for the state of the nation at her alma mater.

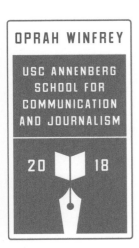

OPRAH WINFREY

USC ANNENBERG
SCHOOL FOR
COMMUNICATION
AND JOURNALISM

20 18

The truth exonerates and it convicts.
It disinfects and it galvanizes. The truth
has always been and will always be our
shield against corruption, our shield
against grief and despair. The truth is
our saving grace.

OPRAH WINFREY (see also page 17) lamented that the Internet and social media are now eroding our trust in institutions but celebrated that each and every one of the graduates would be able to improve the situation in their roles as editorial gatekeepers.

JULIANNA
MARGULIES

Sarah Lawrence
College

———

2010

I have learned to go fully in the face of my dreams. I would recommend you do the same. Now is the time in your life to be selfish. To explore. To take chances. Remember being selfish is not the same as being self-indulgent. You have the gift of time. Use it to do what you love. Believe anything is possible and then work like hell to make it happen.

JULIANNA MARGULIES is an award-winning actress and producer, best known for her roles in the television series *ER* and *The Good Wife*. She returned to her alma mater to give this speech.

DAVID McCULLOUGH JR. | **2012**
Wellesley High School

THE GREAT AND CURIOUS
TRUTH OF THE HUMAN
EXPERIENCE IS THAT
SELFLESSNESS IS THE BEST
THING YOU CAN DO
FOR YOURSELF.

High school teacher **DAVID McCULLOUGH JR.**'s address to his school was called "You Are Not Special," a startling premise for a graduation speech. It was meant to encourage the students to pursue their passion for no other reason than they love it and believe in its importance.

ALAN ALDA

CONNECTICUT COLLEGE

19 80

Be as smart as you can, but remember that it is always better to be wise than to be smart. And don't be upset that it takes a long, long time to find wisdom. Like a rare virus, wisdom tends to break out at unexpected times, and it's mostly people with compassion and understanding who are susceptible to it.

ALAN ALDA is an award-winning actor best known for his roles in *M*A*S*H* and *The West Wing*. He is also a screenwriter, director, and author. When he gave this speech, he addressed his daughter, the first of his three children to graduate from college.

ARIANNA HUFFINGTON
Smith College

2013

WHAT I'M TELLING YOU IS TO REGULARLY DISCONNECT FROM TECHNOLOGY . . . AND RECHARGE IN ORDER TO RECONNECT WITH OURSELVES AND OUR OWN DEEPEST WISDOM . . . WE ALL HAVE WITHIN US A CENTERED PLACE OF WISDOM, HARMONY, AND STRENGTH.

ARIANNA HUFFINGTON (see also page 116), founder of the *Huffington Post* and the tech company Thrive Global, is a *New York Times* bestselling author and syndicated columnist.

10. TIME IS NOT MONEY. TIME IS TIME.

9. TIME IS MORE VALUABLE THAN MONEY.

8. MAGAZINES LARGELY DEVOTED TO REPORTING THE WEIGHT GAINS AND LOSSES OF CELEBRITIES ARE A WASTE OF TIME.

7. ST. AUGUSTINE SAID THAT HE UNDERSTOOD THE CONCEPT OF TIME PERFECTLY UNTIL HE STARTED THINKING ABOUT IT.

6. IN THE PAST, TIME WAS MEASURED NOT IN MONTHS AND HOURS, BUT IN BIRDSONG, THE BRIGHTNESS OF MOONLIGHT, AND THE MIGRATION PATTERNS OF ANIMALS.

5. IN THE WORDS OF JAMES BROWN: "MONEY WON'T CHANGE YOU, BUT TIME WILL TAKE YOU OUT."

4. **WHEN YOUR TIME IS OVER, YOU WILL BE REMEMBERED FOR WHAT YOU DID, NOT FOR WHAT YOU NEVER GOT AROUND TO DOING.**

3. **WHEN YOUR TIME IS DONE, YOU WILL NOT BE REMEMBERED FOR WHAT CLOTHES YOU WORE OR WHAT KIND OF CAR YOU DROVE.**

2. **THERE REALLY IS NO TIME LIKE THE PRESENT. BUT THERE IS NO TIME LIKE THE PAST OR THE FUTURE EITHER, SO WHAT ARE YOU GOING TO DO?**

1. **THE MOST STRIKING DEFINITION OF TIME THAT I KNOW COMES FROM MARTIN AMIS, WHO CALLED TIME "THAT MYSTERIOUS, INEXORABLE FORCE THAT EVENTUALLY WILL MAKE EVERYONE LOOK AND FEEL LIKE HELL."**

MICHAEL
LEWIS

Princeton University

2012

Life's outcomes, while not entirely random, have a huge amount of luck baked into them. Above all, recognize that if you have had success, you have also had luck.

MICHAEL LEWIS is a bestselling author and journalist. His speech outlined the lucky breaks he received after graduating from college, which led to his having a bestseller at age twenty-eight and knowing what career path he wanted.

STEVE BLANK

PHILADELPHIA
UNIVERSITY

20 11

People talk about getting lucky breaks in their careers. I'm living proof that the "lucky breaks" theory is simply wrong. You get to make your own luck. . . . The world is run by those who show up . . . not those who wait to be asked.

Multimillionaire **STEVE BLANK** was a serial entrepreneur involved in the start-ups of eight companies before becoming an author and educator. The college dropout related how his curiosity led him to volunteer for extra work, where he had the opportunity to discover what interested him.

BARBARA KINGSOLVER | 2008

Duke University

QUIT SMOKING AND OBSERVE POSTED SPEED LIMITS. THIS WILL IMPROVE YOUR ODDS OF GETTING OLD ENOUGH TO BE WISE.

BARBARA KINGSOLVER (see page also 94) is a writer of novels, short stories, essays, and other nonfiction. Although she lamented the state of the world in this speech, she titled it "How to Be Hopeful."

SUSAN SONTAG

WELLESLEY COLLEGE

19 83

Lay off the television. And remember, when you hear yourself saying one day that you don't have the time anymore to read—or listen to music, or look at a painting, or go to the movies, or do whatever feeds your head now—then you are getting old. That means they got you after all.

SUSAN SONTAG was a writer and intellectual best known for her essays on modern culture. She also wrote novels and plays and was a filmmaker, teacher, philosopher, and political activist.

ELLEN DeGENERES

Tulane University

———

2009

For me, the most important thing in your life is to . . . follow your passion, stay true to yourself. Never follow anyone else's path, unless you're in the woods and you're lost and you see a path and by all means you should follow that.

ELLEN DeGENERES is a comedian, television producer, and LGBTQ+ icon. In her address, she recounted her early successes and then what happened to her when she publicly came out as gay: for three years, she had no employment. But DeGeneres said she wouldn't change a thing.

KATIE COURIC
Williams College

| 2007

THE ROAD LESS TRAVELED IS SOMETIMES FRAUGHT WITH BARRICADES, BUMPS, AND UNCHARTED TERRAIN. BUT IT IS ON THAT ROAD WHERE YOUR CHARACTER IS TRULY TESTED— AND YOUR PERSONAL GROWTH REALIZED.

KATIE COURIC is a journalist, author, and television host who became the first woman to solo anchor a national broadcast news program.

GWEN IFILL

SIMMONS
COLLEGE

19 93

Life is all about choices. . . .
You now face the most staggering
array of choices that you may ever
have before you in your life. Do not
underestimate their range. . . .
Take every choice you are offered.
Have as much fun as you can,
when you can. Do not shrink from
life, and do not shrink from choices.

GWEN IFILL was a journalist, newscaster, and author. In 1999, she was the first Black woman to host a nationally televised news program, *Washington Week in Review*.

TERRY
TEMPEST
WILLIAMS

College of the Atlantic

1999

See, feel, question, explore, experience, walk, dance, run, play, eat, love, learn, dare, taste, touch, smell, listen, argue, speak, write, read, draw, provoke, emote, scream, cry, kneel, pray, pray often, bow, rise, stand, look, sing, embrace the questions, be wary of answers, create, cajole, confront, confound, walk backward, walk forward, circle, hide, seek, say no, say yes, embrace, follow your heart, trust your heart, engage love again and again on this beautiful, broken world.

TERRY TEMPEST WILLIAMS is a writer, educator, conservationist, and activist whose writings are rooted in the American West, especially in the arid lands of Utah. She is a recipient of the Sierra Club's John Muir Award.

KURT VONNEGUT | 1999

Agnes Scott College

WE CAN LEARN TO LIVE
WITHOUT THE SICK EXCITEMENT,
WITHOUT THE KICK OF HAVING
SCORES TO SETTLE WITH THIS
PARTICULAR PERSON, OR THAT
BUNCH OF PEOPLE, OR THAT
PARTICULAR INSTITUTION
OR RACE OR NATION.

KURT VONNEGUT was a novelist, essayist, playwright, and screenwriter with a satirical style and a penchant for science fiction. A collection of nine of his commencement speeches, titled *If This Isn't Nice, What Is? Advice to the Young,* was published posthumously in 2013.

ELIZABETH
WARREN

Suffolk University

2016

Knowing who you are will help you when it's time to fight. Fight for the job you want, fight for the people who mean the most to you, and fight for the kind of world you want to live in.

ELIZABETH WARREN is a lawyer, an author, and a politician representing Massachusetts as a United States senator since 2013. She was formerly a law professor, specializing in bankruptcy law. In her speech, Warren drew from her own experiences to support her advice.

RUSSELL BAKER

Connecticut College

1995

1. BEND DOWN ONCE IN A WHILE AND SMELL A FLOWER.

2. DON'T GO AROUND IN CLOTHES THAT TALK.

3. LISTEN ONCE IN A WHILE.

4. SLEEP IN THE NUDE.

5. TURN OFF THE TV ONCE OR TWICE A MONTH AND PICK UP A BOOK.

6 *DON'T TAKE YOUR GUN TO TOWN.*

7 *LEARN TO FEAR THE AUTOMOBILE.*

8 *HAVE SOME CHILDREN.*

9 *GET MARRIED.*

10 *SMILE.*

RUSSELL BAKER was a columnist, author, humorist, and political satirist. Although he advised those going out into the messy world not to do it, he offered ten ways to help avoid making the world even worse.

ANGELA DAVIS
Grinnell University

2007

I WANT TO HELP YOU RETRIEVE, AND SORT THROUGH, AND RETHINK, AND INDEED PRESERVE MEMORIES OF WHAT MAY WELL TURN OUT TO BE THE MOST IMPORTANT PERIOD OF YOUR LIVES.

ANGELA DAVIS is a political activist, academic, and writer. Known internationally, Davis advocates for gender and race equality and criminal justice reform.

OCTAVIA
SPENCER

KENT STATE
UNIVERSITY

20 17

Now, there may be a temptation to think that these were the best years of your lives because of everything and everyone you discovered here. But that would be too narrow a vision, too myopic. I promise you that everyone here has been a part of shaping you for a future you could never have dreamt for yourself.

OCTAVIA SPENCER is an actress and producer who won an Oscar and a Golden Globe Award for her role in the film *The Help*. She is also the author of a children's fiction series.

I've found that nothing in life is worthwhile unless you take risks. . . . If I'm going to fall . . . I want to fall forward. . . . Reggie Jackson struck out 2,600 times in his career—the most in the history of baseball. But you don't hear about the strikeouts. People remember the home runs. Fall forward. Thomas Edison conducted 1,000 failed experiments. Did you know that? I didn't either—because number 1,001 was the light bulb. Fall forward. Every failed experiment is one step closer to success.

Two-time Academy Award winner **DENZEL WASHINGTON** is an actor, director, and producer who has also won Tony and Golden Globe awards. In this speech, he gave examples of overcoming his own failures, first in school, and then in his career.

CONAN O'BRIEN

DARTMOUTH COLLEGE

20 11

A little over a year ago I experienced a profound and very public disappointment. . . . To this day I still don't understand exactly what happened, but I have never had more fun, been more challenged—and this is important—had more conviction about what I was doing. How could this be true? Well, it's simple: There are few things more liberating in this life than having your worst fear realized.

CONAN O'BRIEN is a writer, comedian, producer, and television talk show host who was removed from his dream job at *The Tonight Show*. In his commencement speech to the Dartmouth graduates he shared valuable lessons from that experience.

BARBARA
KINGSOLVER

DUKE
UNIVERSITY

20 08

What if someone had dared you, three years ago, to show up to some public event wearing a big, flappy dress with sleeves down to your knees. And on your head, oh, let's say, a beanie with a square board on top. And a tassel! Look at you. You are beautiful. The magic is community. . . . The ridiculously earnest are known to travel in groups. And they are known to change the world.

Writer **BARBARA KINGSOLVER** (see also page 80) is a popular commencement speaker. She delivers serious material in an appealing and often humorous way.

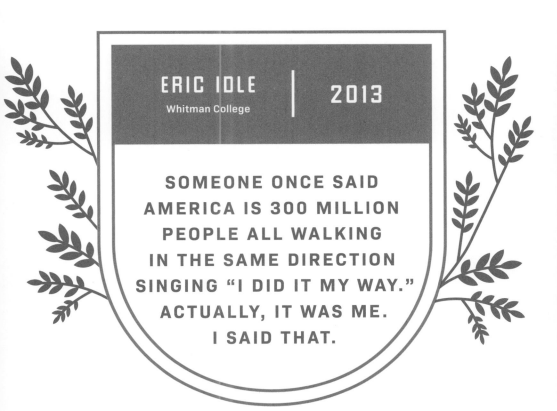

ERIC IDLE | 2013
Whitman College

SOMEONE ONCE SAID
AMERICA IS 300 MILLION
PEOPLE ALL WALKING
IN THE SAME DIRECTION
SINGING "I DID IT MY WAY."
ACTUALLY, IT WAS ME.
I SAID THAT.

ERIC IDLE (see also page 117) describes himself on Twitter as a "writer, reader, husband, father, Dogfather, dog owner, guitarist, humorist, humanist, satirist, cricket fan." He is a founding member of Monty Python and creator of the musical *Spamalot*.

NEIL GAIMAN

University of the Arts

———

2012

Something that worked for me was imagining that where I wanted to be—an author, primarily of fiction, making good books, making good comics, and supporting myself through my words—was a mountain. . . . as long as I kept walking towards the mountain I would be all right. And when I truly was not sure what to do, I could think about whether it was taking me towards or away from the mountain. I said no to editorial jobs because I knew that would have been walking away from the mountain.

NEIL GAIMAN (see also page 46) admitted he never could have seen himself giving advice to graduates because he never had graduated himself, escaping as soon as he could to pursue what he wanted to do. At the age of fifteen, he wrote a list and then proceeded to check off each entry.

JOYCE DiDONATO
The Juilliard School

2014

ONE OF THE GREATEST GIFTS YOU CAN GIVE YOURSELF, RIGHT HERE, RIGHT NOW, IN THIS SINGLE, SOLITARY, MONUMENTAL MOMENT IN YOUR LIFE, IS TO DECIDE, WITHOUT APOLOGY, TO COMMIT TO THE JOURNEY, AND NOT TO THE OUTCOME.

Mezzo-soprano **JOYCE DIDONATO** has performed with many of the world's leading opera companies and orchestras. She is the winner of three Grammy Awards and the 2018 Olivier Award for Outstanding Achievement in Opera.

TIM MINCHIN

The University of
Western Australia

2013

1. **YOU DON'T HAVE TO HAVE A DREAM.**
   I advocate passionate dedication to the
   pursuit of short-term goals.

2. **DON'T SEEK HAPPINESS.**
   Happiness is like an orgasm. If you think
   about it too much it goes away.

3. **REMEMBER, IT'S ALL LUCK.**
   Understanding that you can't truly take
   credit for your successes nor truly blame
   others for their failures will humble you
   and make you more compassionate.

4. **EXERCISE.**
   You think, therefore you are. . . . But
   also: you jog, therefore you sleep well,
   therefore you're not overwhelmed by
   existential angst.

5. **BE HARD ON YOUR OPINIONS.**
   We must think critically, and not just about the ideas of others. Be hard on your beliefs.

6. **BE A TEACHER!**
   Rejoice in what you learn, and spray it.

7. **DEFINE YOURSELF BY WHAT YOU LOVE.**
   Be pro-stuff, not just anti-stuff.

8. **RESPECT PEOPLE WITH LESS POWER THAN YOU.**
   I don't care if you're the most powerful cat in the room, I will judge you on how you treat the least powerful.

9. **FINALLY, DON'T RUSH.**
   Most people I know who were sure of their career path at twenty are having midlife crises now.

TIM MINCHIN is a composer, musician, lyricist, comedian, actor, writer, and director whose *Matilda the Musical* won a record seven Olivier Awards. Minchin was appointed a Member of the Order of Australia in 2020 for his contributions to the performing arts and the community. He offered these nine life lessons to graduates at the University of Western Australia.

STUDS TERKEL

GRINNELL COLLEGE

19 77

If we have no sense of history, how can we recognize the challenge of now unless we remember the challenges of then? And when they say let's forget the past, let bygones be bygones, we must remember to say no. . . . When they say let's put all our dark side behind, we must remember to say no so that we can better see the light that is within all of us.

STUDS TERKEL was a Pulitzer Prize–winning author and oral historian who chronicled the lives of what he called the "uncelebrated" working class. In his writings he concentrated on American life in the twentieth century.

BROOKE L. BLOWER

Boston University

2013

History can give us courage and a sense of proportion. It can teach us to move beyond ourselves and envision other worlds, to put ourselves in others' shoes. It teaches us to be suspicious of easy answers, to understand the role of chance, but also to recognize the ways in which individuals continue to make a major impact. . . . It enables us to see all the ways in which those things we take for granted as natural and normal—as just the way things are—are not, in fact, timeless. And if you recognize that the world is something that has changed, you will see more clearly how it can be changed again.

BROOKE L. BLOWER is a professor and author and editor of books and articles on history. This commencement address was given at the history department convocation.

KRISTEN BELL

USC SCHOOL OF DRAMATIC ARTS

20 19

When you really listen to people, when you listen as fiercely as you want to be heard, when you respect the idea that you are sharing the earth with other humans, when you lead with your nice foot forward, you'll win every time.

KRISTEN BELL is an actress known for her roles in *Veronica Mars, The Good Place,* and *Frozen.* In her speech, she shared the secret that she never graduated from college. She admitted, however, that she is nice, which makes people overlook a lot.

ANNA QUINDLEN

GRINNELL
COLLEGE

20 11

The voices of conformity speak so loudly. Don't listen to them. People are going to tell you what you ought to think and how you ought to feel. They will tell you what to read and how to live. They will urge you to take jobs they loathe themselves and to follow safe paths that they themselves find tedious. Don't do it.

ANNA QUINDLEN (see also pages 21 and 65) was confident that the graduates could remake the country stronger and smarter by applying the critical thinking they had learned.

HANK
AZARIA

Tufts University

2016

One day, a very powerful director can walk up to you and tell you to lower your voice, and if you do it, you will win an Oscar. And on another day, that very same director can walk up to you and tell you to lower your voice and if you don't do it, you will win an Oscar. Now, how will you know which is the right decision? You know, in a moment like that, what you think anybody else might do will not help you. But . . . if you calm down, you will know what your instincts are telling you and you'll know which way, right or wrong, that you must proceed.

HANK AZARIA is an actor, singer, comedian, and producer probably best known for his voice characterizations on the animated sitcom *The Simpsons*. In some of his speech to the graduates of his alma mater, he gave advice in the voices of his beloved characters from the TV show.

JENNIFER
LEE

University of
New Hampshire

2014

When you are free from self-doubt, you fail better, because you don't have your defenses up, you can accept the criticism. You don't become so preoccupied with that failure that you forget how to learn from it, you forget how to grow. When you believe in yourself, you succeed better. Hours spent questioning, doubting, fearing, can be given over to working, exploring, living.

Oscar-winner **JENNIFER LEE** is a screenwriter, film director, and the chief creative officer of Walt Disney Animation Studios. She is best known for her work on *Frozen, Frozen 2,* and *Wreck-It Ralph.*

JOHN McCAIN

OHIO WESLEYAN
UNIVERSITY

20 10

I have faith that you understand that assaults on the dignity of others are assaults on the dignity of all humanity. You will not look upon tyranny and injustice in faraway places as the inevitable tragedy of mankind's fallen nature. You will see them as a call to action.

JOHN McCAIN was a much-awarded military officer who entered politics after his service. He endured six years in North Vietnam as a prisoner of war and went on to become a United States senator from Arizona. McCain ran for president against Barack Obama in 2008.

ANNE
MARIE
SLAUGHTER

Washington
University in St. Louis

2018

Your mission . . . is American renewal. . . . Go back to your hometowns, state capitals, or bustling regional cities. . . . Go to where you can participate in the reconnection of citizen action to positive public outcomes.
It's the American way.

ANNE MARIE SLAUGHTER is an international lawyer, political scientist, analyst, and commentator. She has taught at several colleges, served as the first woman director of policy planning for the State Department, and is now CEO of New America, a nonprofit think and action tank.

GIVE ME

GIVE ME THE EFFING JOB.

GIVE ME THE SAME PAY THAT THE GUY NEXT TO ME GETS.

GIVE ME THE PROMOTION.

GIVE ME THE MICROPHONE.

GIVE ME THE OVAL OFFICE.

GIVE ME THE RESPECT I'VE EARNED

AND GIVE IT TO MY WOLF PACK, TOO.

THE EFFING BALL.

ABBY WAMBACH is a soccer superstar, a two-time Olympic gold medalist, and a FIFA Women's World Cup champion, as well as an advocate for equal rights for women.

SPIKE LEE
Johns Hopkins University | 2016

NOW'S THE TIME TO SEIZE THE DAY, TAKE ADVANTAGE OF THIS UNIQUE MOMENT IN HISTORY, AND BUILD BRIDGES AMONGST US. TALKING ABOUT GENDER, RACE, RELIGION, AND NATIONS, NOT WALLS. LET US BUILD BRIDGES OF LOVE, VERSUS WALLS OF HATE.

SPIKE LEE is a film director, producer, writer, actor, and professor whose works include *Do the Right Thing, Jungle Fever,* and *BlacKKKlansman.* His provocative speech urged graduates to make a better world for the ninety-nine percent.

BILLY
COLLINS

Colorado College

2008

The corollary to carpe diem
is gratitude, gratitude
for simply being alive,
for having a day to seize.

BILLY COLLINS (see also page 76) served as United States Poet Laureate from 2001 to 2003 and taught at Lehman College in the City University of New York for almost fifty years.

CHRISTIAN LOUBOUTIN

FASHION INSTITUTE OF TECHNOLOGY

20 14

You are at a very specific time of age... an age where you can follow all your dreams. But also at an age when you can change—you can change your dreams, you can change paths. When you start something when you're young, you should not decide "This is it, this is my way and I will go all the way." You have the age where you can change. You get experience, and maybe dislike it and go another way. Your age is still an age of exploration.

CHRISTIAN LOUBOUTIN is a French footwear designer known for his high-heeled shoes with a signature red sole. He meandered from job to job in his early years, following positions that interested him. He encouraged graduates to do the same.

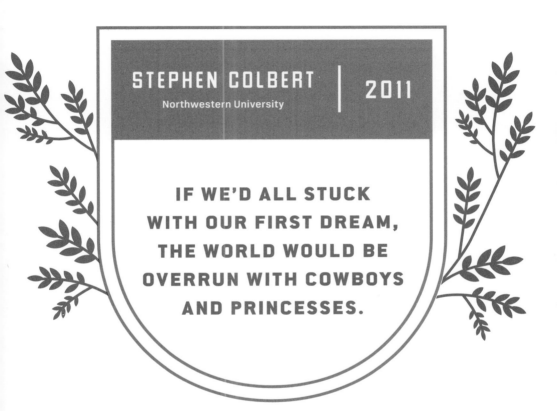

STEPHEN COLBERT | 2011
Northwestern University

IF WE'D ALL STUCK
WITH OUR FIRST DREAM,
THE WORLD WOULD BE
OVERRUN WITH COWBOYS
AND PRINCESSES.

STEPHEN COLBERT (see also page 10) returned to his school twenty-five years later to talk about important lessons he had learned: life is like an improvisation, in that you don't know what is happening next and you make it up as you go along. He also learned that dreams can change.

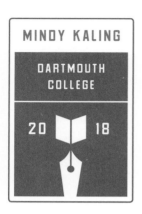

I was not someone who should have the life I have now, and yet I do. I was sitting in the chair you are literally sitting in right now and I just whispered, "Why not me?" And I kept whispering it for seventeen years; and here I am. . . . Don't let anyone tell you that you can't do something, but especially not yourself. Go conquer the world.

MINDY KALING is a comedian, actress, writer, and producer. A collection of her humorous essays, *Why Not Me?*, published in 2015, was a bestseller.

DAVID
FOSTER
WALLACE

Kenyon College

———

2005

It is extremely difficult to stay alert and attentive, instead of getting hypnotized by the constant monologue inside your own head (may be happening right now). Twenty years after my own graduation, I have come gradually to understand that the liberal arts cliché about teaching you how to think is actually shorthand for a much deeper, more serious idea: learning how to think really means learning how to exercise some control over how and what you think.

DAVID FOSTER WALLACE was a writer of fiction and nonfiction and a professor. He claimed the value of education was not knowledge as much as the simple awareness of the world around you. This speech was made into a book, *This Is Water*.

ARIANNA HUFFINGTON

VASSAR COLLEGE

20 15

We have, if we're lucky, about thirty thousand days to play the game of life. And trust me, that's not morbid. In fact, it's wisdom that will put all the inevitable failures and rejections and disappointments and heartbreaks into perspective.

ARIANNA HUFFINGTON (see also page 75) advised graduates to introduce digital detoxes into their life, to not be so connected to everybody that they're not connected to anybody, including themselves, and to take time to be present, bringing joy and gratitude to every moment.

ERIC IDLE | 2013

Whitman College

LIFE HAS A VERY SIMPLE PLOT. FIRST YOU'RE HERE, AND THEN YOU'RE NOT.

ERIC IDLE (see also page 95) lived up to his Monty Python persona in his hilarious address to his daughter's graduation class. Idle even assured the audience regarding the Second Amendment that there was no need for many muskets: the Brits weren't coming back.

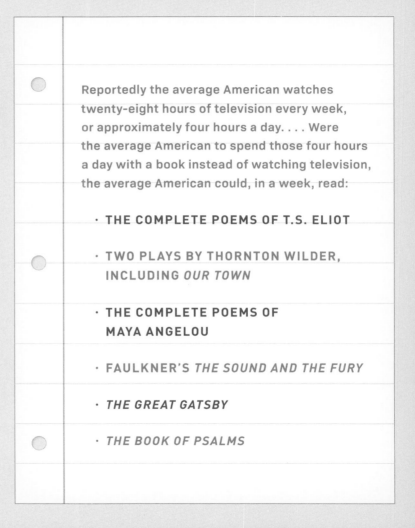

Reportedly the average American watches
twenty-eight hours of television every week,
or approximately four hours a day. . . . Were
the average American to spend those four hours
a day with a book instead of watching television,
the average American could, in a week, read:

- **THE COMPLETE POEMS OF T.S. ELIOT**

- **TWO PLAYS BY THORNTON WILDER,
  INCLUDING** *OUR TOWN*

- **THE COMPLETE POEMS OF
  MAYA ANGELOU**

- **FAULKNER'S** *THE SOUND AND THE FURY*

- *THE GREAT GATSBY*

- *THE BOOK OF PSALMS*

READ, READ, READ,

IS MY COMMENCEMENT ADVICE.

Historian **DAVID McCULLOUGH** has twice received both the Pulitzer Prize and the National Book Award. He has also been the recipient of the Presidential Medal of Freedom. He characterized himself as an English major who happened into history and a reader who decided to write the kinds of books he liked to read.

WYNTON MARSALIS

University of Vermont

———

2013

It's harder to build than destroy. To build is to engage and change. . . . Changes are like obstacles on a speed course. They demand your attention and require you to be present. They are coming, they are here, and then they are gone. It's how life comes. Each moment is a procession from the future into the past and the sweet spot is always the present.

WYNTON MARSALIS is a musician, a composer, the artistic director of Jazz at Lincoln Center, and the first jazz musician to win the Pulitzer Prize for Music. He has won many awards for his jazz and classical music, expanding the vocabulary of both in inventive ways.

BRIAN KENNY

OHIO NORTHERN UNIVERSITY

20 07

There's no "there" there. . . .
That elusive "there" with the job,
the beach house, the dream, it's not
out there. "There" is here. . . . That
real happiness, real contentment
has to be IN you regardless of
professional achievement and
amount of wealth. . . . You are
THERE, now. . . . Remember this,
THERE is here, breathe deep,
you're there. Savor this moment.

BRIAN KENNY is an Emmy Award–winning broadcaster and host for the MLB Network. He is a proponent of sabermetrics and baseball analytics. Kenny is also a blow-by-blow boxing announcer for Fox Sports.

TOM HANKS

Virtual Speech
to Wright State
University

—

2020

You started [college] in the olden times, in the world back before the great pandemic of 2020. . . . You'll reference these past weeks . . . as during the pandemic . . . you will continue on into the after, as in that was after the virus was tamed. . . . But your after is not going to look the same as your during or as your before. You will have seen the movie and you will know how it ends.

You will have made it through the time of great sacrifice and great need, and no one will be more fresh to the task of restarting our measure of normalcy than you. . . . You are going to form the new structures and define the new realities and make the new world, the world after all that we have been through.

The future is always uncertain, but . . . we are certain . . . you will not let us down.

Two-time Oscar-winning actor **TOM HANKS** and his wife Rita Wilson were some of the first well-known people to contract the coronavirus during the 2020 COVID-19 pandemic. Hanks' recovery gave added poignancy to this virtual commencement speech.

BARACK OBAMA

Virtual Speech
to High School
Graduates

2020

I won't tell you what to do with this power that rests in your hands. But I'll leave you with three quick pieces of advice.

First, don't be afraid. America's gone through tough times before... And each time we came out stronger, usually because a new generation... learned from past mistakes and figured out how to make things better.

Second, do what you think is right.... ground yourself in values that last, like honesty, hard work, responsibility, fairness, generosity, respect for others.

And finally, build a community.... Stand up for one another's rights. Leave behind all the old ways of thinking that divide us—sexism, racial prejudice, status, greed—and set the world on a different path.

One high school senior tweeted at former President **BARACK OBAMA** (see also page 16), asking if he would give a national commencement speech. The tweet went viral and Obama ended up giving two speeches, one addressed to Historic Black Colleges and Universities and the other to high school graduates.

CALL YOUR MOM AND DAD ONCE IN A WHILE. A TIME WILL COME WHEN YOU WILL WANT YOUR OWN GROWN-UP, BUSY, HYPER-SUCCESSFUL CHILDREN TO CALL YOU. ALSO, REMEMBER WHO PAID YOUR TUITION.

BEN BERNANKE is an economist at the Brookings Institution and former chair of the Federal Reserve Bank from 2006 to 2014. This advice was the last in a list of ten suggestions that had been "road-tested in real-life situations."

MERYL STREEP
Barnard College

2010

YOU DON'T HAVE TO BE FAMOUS. YOU JUST HAVE TO MAKE YOUR MOTHER AND FATHER PROUD OF YOU AND YOU ALREADY HAVE.

MERYL STREEP is an actress, nominated for a record twenty-one Academy Awards and winner of three.

INDEX

Published in the United States by Clarkson Potter/Publishers, an
imprint of Random House, a division of Penguin Random House
LLC, New York.
clarksonpotter.com

CLARKSON POTTER is a trademark and POTTER with colophon is a
registered trademark of Penguin Random House LLC.

ISBN 978-0-593-13975-2

Printed in China

Design by Lise Sukhu

10 9 8 7 6 5 4 3 2

First Edition

NEVER HAS A GRADUATING
CLASS BEEN CALLED TO STEP
INTO THE FUTURE WITH MORE
PURPOSE, VISION, PASSION AND
ENERGY AND HOPE.

—

OPRAH WINFREY

CARE SELFLESSLY
ABOUT ONE
ANOTHER.

—

DR. ANTHONY FAUCI

Let no opportunity be
too small for your time,
let no opportunity be too big
for your possibilities.

—

JON STEWART

IT'S NOT
ABOUT YOU.

—

DAVID CHANG